Natural Resources

by Greg Underhill

 HOUGHTON MIFFLIN   BOSTON

Contents

Trees are a natural resource.

Introduction

Natural resources are things that we find in nature that we can use. Some natural resources are water, trees, minerals, sunlight, and wind. We drink water. We use trees to make houses and paper. We dig minerals out of the ground and use them to make metals. Then we use the metals to make machines. We use the sun and the wind as energy to make the machines go.

Chapter 1
Kinds of Natural Resources

Some natural resources are living things. Animals, trees, and plants are living natural resources. We use plants and animals as food. We need these natural resources to live. We also use animals to help us. All living things need natural resources such as air, water, and sunlight.

This is an oil field. Oil is a natural resource.

We will never use up air, water, and sunlight. But we can use up other natural resources. Oil is a natural resource. We use oil in many different ways. We use it to heat our homes, make our cars go, and make plastic things. Someday we may use up all of the oil in the world.

Nonrenewable Resources

Oil is called a nonrenewable natural resource. We cannot make more of a nonrenewable resource after it is gone. Oil comes from deep in the ground. Oil is called a fossil fuel. Fossil fuels were made from plants and animals that died a long time ago. It takes millions of years for oil to form. Some scientists think we will use up all the oil in the world in fewer than 100 years.

Oil: How Much We Make and How Much We Use

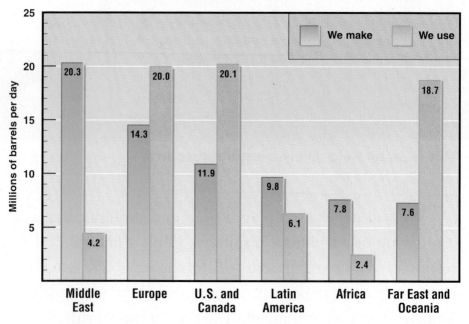

Trees grow back after a forest fire in Yellowstone National Park.

Renewable Resources

Trees are renewable resources. We can make more of a renewable resource. When we cut down a tree, we can plant a new tree. We will never run out of trees if we continue to plant new ones.

The Water Cycle

Water is a renewable resource. We can use water over and over again. The earth always has the same amount of water. Water is used over and over again because of the water cycle. In the water cycle, the sun makes the water in the ocean evaporate. When the water evaporates, it changes into vapor. Vapor is a gas. The water vapor turns into clouds. The wind carries the clouds over the land.

We will always have the same amount of water because of the water cycle.

The Water Cycle

condensation

precipitation

evaporation

collection

The water vapor in the clouds turns to water. The water is called condensation. The condensation becomes raindrops. The raindrops fall to the earth. Rain is called precipitation. The precipitation fills lakes and ponds. It falls on the land, travels through the ground, and fills underground wells. The rainwater goes into rivers and streams. It also goes back into the oceans. Then the water cycle begins again.

Making Good Use of Resources

We have to take care of all our natural resources, even renewable resources. Sometimes people throw garbage and poisons into the lakes and oceans. The water becomes dirty. We say the water is polluted. If people do not plant new trees after they cut down old trees, we will not have forests.

People put water filled with poisons into a river in Mexico City, Mexico.

Some natural resources are nonrenewable, but we can recycle them. We can use recycled resources again and again. We can recycle many different kinds of metals. Aluminum is a metal. We can use aluminum over and over again.

Recycling

Do you recycle empty soda cans? Soda cans are made of aluminum. Many people take the aluminum cans to a recycling center. The used cans get made into new cans.

We can recycle aluminum things many times. If we recycle, we will always have enough aluminum.

Aluminum cans at a recycling center

We can also recycle plastics, paper, and glass. We have to recycle. If we do not recycle, we will use up many metals. We will fill up all the garbage dumps, or landfills. When you throw something away, think about it. Where will the trash go? Can you recycle it?

Chapter 2
Natural Resources of the United States

There are many natural resources in the United States. We make many things from our natural resources. Some important natural resources are coal, iron ore, natural gas, oil, copper, gold, silver, and lead. The most important resource in the United States is land.

Mount Moran and Jackson Lake in Grand Teton National Park, Wyoming

Farmers grow wheat in the midwestern part of the United States.

Our Soil

Land with good soil is an important natural resource. The United States has some of the best soil in the world. Farmers can grow many different kinds of crops in this good soil. In the midwestern part of the United States, farmers grow plenty of wheat and corn. They sell these crops to people in many parts of the world.

Our Water and Forests

Water is another important natural resource of the United States. The United States has lots of lakes and rivers, so we have a lot of fresh water. We use about 400 billion (400,000,000,000) gallons of water every day. 400 billion gallons is equal to the water in 16 billion (16,000,000,000) swimming pools used in Olympic Games! Farms and factories use most of this water.

Fresh water at Yosemite National Park, California

A forest in Muir Woods National Monument, California

The forests of the United States are another important natural resource. There are forests in about one-third (1/3) of our country. We use the wood from the trees for building. This wood is called lumber. We get a lot of lumber from forests in the northwestern part of the United States. We get wood pulp to make paper from forests in the South and the Northeast. We use wood from the Appalachian forests and the Great Lakes area to make tables, chairs, desks, and other furniture.

Our Fish

Fish are also an important natural resource of the United States. There are about five million (5,000,000) fish caught in the United States every year. Most of this fish comes from the Pacific Ocean. In the Pacific Ocean, people catch salmon, tuna, and crabs. In the Gulf of Mexico, people catch oysters and shrimp. In the Atlantic Ocean, they catch flounder, cod, and lobsters. Catching too many fish can cause a problem. This is called overfishing. We overfish when we catch more fish than nature can replace. Then we have fewer fish to eat. Also, large fish have fewer fish to eat.

Fishermen catch salmon.

President Theodore Roosevelt and John Muir in Yosemite National Park, 1903

Chapter 3
Saving Our Natural Resources

In the 1900s, people in the United States started to take care of, or protect, natural resources. Protecting natural resources is called conservation. President Theodore Roosevelt wanted to protect the forests, and the lakes and rivers. He gave land in the western part of the United States to the government. The forests became national forests. The U.S. government still protects these national forests.

Other people wanted to protect the forests, lakes, and rivers. For example, John Muir loved nature. John Muir went to Alaska and found a glacier. A glacier is a very big mass of ice that slowly moves over land. This glacier was named after John Muir. Muir Woods, an area of redwood trees in California, was also named after him. John Muir traveled all over the country. He often traveled by walking. He wrote books about his travels. John Muir liked President Roosevelt's work for conservation.

Giant redwood trees in the Muir Woods National Monument, California

These young people are helping to conserve the land.

Today, conservation is important to many people. Some people want to have beautiful trees and lakes. Others work to protect the air and water. Farmers want to protect the soil. They want to continue to plant crops. In the United States, most people think that conservation is important.

Sometimes it is difficult to protect the land and to do the right thing for the people who live there. Sometimes people want to use the land for other things, but they cannot. They cannot use the land because protected animals or plants live there. The land might have other protected resources too. People do not always agree about the best way to use the land.

This person wants to protect the forest.

Earth

There are more and more people in the world every day. Today there are about six billion (6,000,000,000) people on earth. By the year 2050, there may be 10 billion (10,000,000,000) people. There will be more people using natural resources. We have to think about the best way to use and protect our natural resources. Our decisions now will affect people in the future.

Glossary

condensation water vapor that changes from a gas to a liquid, such as raindrops in a cloud

conservation protecting natural resources

evaporate to change from a liquid to a gas. For example, the water in the ocean evaporates and forms clouds.

natural resources things found in nature that we can use. For example, we use water, trees, and minerals.

nonrenewable resources resources that we use up faster than nature can replace them

renewable resources resources that nature can replace

water cycle the recycling of water from the ocean to clouds to precipitation into lakes and rivers and back to the ocean again